Feelings

How are you feeling today? When you were really small, you could only tell
if you felt good or you felt bad. That's why you cried when you were hungry or
your tummy ached. Now you are big and you no longer cry when you
are hungry, because you have learned that the feeling goes away
if you eat something.

2

As you grow bigger, you will learn a lot about feelings, because growing up is a great adventure in which you are always learning new things!

3

Do you remember when you were in your mom's belly? Maybe you could already feel all the love your parents had for you, even when they had not seen you yet! Love is so big and so intense that it covers everything. It's bigger than a house, the sea...it's even bigger than the whole universe!

There are different ways to love. You love your parents in a different way than you love a friend, and the way you love a cat or a flower is not the same as the way you love your grandpa and grandma!

5

It's nighttime, your parents have gone to bed, and you are alone in your room. It's dark and you can hear thunder outside. Kabooooooooom! You're afraid! Or maybe you have had a nightmare. Try to get up from bed and turn on the light. It's not so bad with the light on, is it?

We can be afraid of many different things, but that should not worry you. Things that make you afraid now will disappear—never to return—as you grow bigger.

7

Have you ever been lost? You feel alone and abandoned, nobody you know is around, you can't see your parents. That's terrible! But even in a situation like this, you must know that your parents have not left you behind and are looking for you at this very moment. They'll find you right away, you'll see!

When this happens, your parents also feel very afraid, so they'll hug you and kiss you many times when they finally find you. Or they may even scold you , but who cares? Phew! You've found them!

9

Have you ever seen fireworks? It is surprising to see so many bright little lights of different colors bursting in the air. Everybody's eyes are wide open and everyone goes "Oooooh!" This is the face we make when we have a surprise.

At first, the noise is a little frightening, but the show is worth it!

Having a little brother is fun, but sometimes you feel your parents pay more attention to him than to you. Then you feel a little angry, and maybe also a little sad and...then you feel you don't like your little brother.

Have you ever thought the same thing could happen to him when he grows older?

12

The love of your parents is so big that they can love you and all your brothers and sisters as well, even if you had two hundred!
To them, you are unique, special, and marvelous just the way you are!

13

There are days when everything is just great fun. You feel happy and laugh all the time. It's like going to a theme park and having as many rides as you want on your favorite attractions.

14

Have you noticed what people do when they
are happy? They laugh, sing, dance....
Everything seems easier to do,
even boring tasks like
putting your toys away!

15

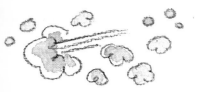

You are angry because your friend has ruined your beautiful drawing. But that's not all. When he sees that you are mad at him, he just laughs and calls you names. It makes you so mad! But don't let your anger get the best of you. You could do things you might regret later.

Whenever you feel very, very angry, the best thing you can do is go out for a walk, or stay in your room playing alone or reading a story. After all, a friend is more important than a drawing, right?

17

What makes you feel ashamed? Maybe not
knowing how to ride a bike, or wetting
your bed when you are asleep...there are
so many things that can make a person
feel ashamed! Feeling ashamed is very
uncomfortable, because then you cannot
have fun.

18

The adults you love may tell you what made them feel
ashamed when they were your age. Who knows,
you might find out they were a lot like you!

There are things you don't like at all: people who aren't nice, food that tastes horrible, smells that make you wrinkle your nose. There are really some things you strongly dislike. Just imagining them makes you sick!

Maybe if you try them several times, you'll get used to some of them. You may even be surprised to find out they aren't as bad as you thought! Want to give them a try?

21

Sometimes things happen that make you feel sad. At times sadness grows so much inside you that it finally overflows in the form of tears. Can you notice how they taste? They taste salty. Tears are good because they help you to drive your sadness away!

The best way to spill out all your sadness is to share what you feel with someone you love. A warm hug can work miracles!

After your bath, when you get out of the tub, your dad wraps you in a big fluffy towel and carries you in his arms, tickling you all the time. After you have your pajamas on, he tells you a new and fantastic story.
You feel so happy!

24

There are many happy moments in life.
You feel like the sun is inside you, making
everything around you shine and glow.
It is a wonderful feeling!

You have been afraid, sad, angry, happy....
You have had a lot of feelings! Now you
have an idea how you feel and how others feel.
Maybe you can even keep a friend company
when he is afraid or comfort him when
he feels sad!

Try to comfort someone and you will feel good and very grown up. That's what your parents do with you!

27

All of us are different and that's why we all feel things differently. Even you change your mood according to the way you feel: when you are angry, nothing seems to be funny. When you are happy, however, you just laugh at anything. Can you imagine how boring it would be if everything were always the same?

Every feeling you have helps you to know the world around you. That's how you grow up!

Activiti**e**s

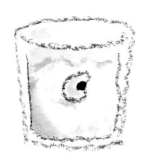

What a surprise

Walking through the woods, you find a colorful berry, an appetizing chestnut, or a squirrel watching you from up a tree. The world is full of such surprises, and many people react with a growing love for nature. How about loving a plant right at home?

Get a bean, wrap it in wet cotton, and place it in a glass pot. Keep the pot where there is plenty of light (but not in the sun) and just wait. The only thing you have to do is keep the cotton wet by adding a little water every day. And a few days later...surprise! A plant will start growing. When its leaves are big and green, transfer it to a flowerpot full of soil, so the plant will grow big and strong. Don't you love your little plant?

Who is who?

Have you ever tried hiding a lot of people in a single room? One of the players stays out of the room while the others try to hide as well as they can. When everybody is ready, someone turns off the light and calls the outside player in. The room has to be in complete darkness so he/she cannot see anyone. The player goes around the room, trying to find the other players one by one and guessing who is who by touching their faces and hair. No tickling allowed!

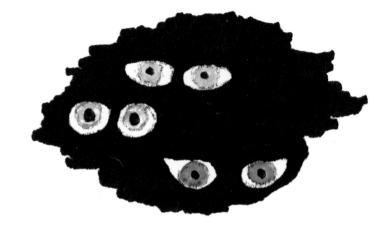

Dice of feelings

Ask an adult to make you a big die like this one. You can help by cutting out and gluing the different parts. You need only some cardboard or oaktag, scissors, glue, and a little bit of patience!

Write the name of a feeling on each side of the die: fear, anger, happiness, sadness, shame... . You can make as many dice as you wish and you only need to think of which feeling you will write on each side.

Now you are ready to play with your family or a group of friends. Sit forming a circle and throw the dice, taking turns. Each player will describe a moment when he/she experienced the feeling written on the top of the die.

31

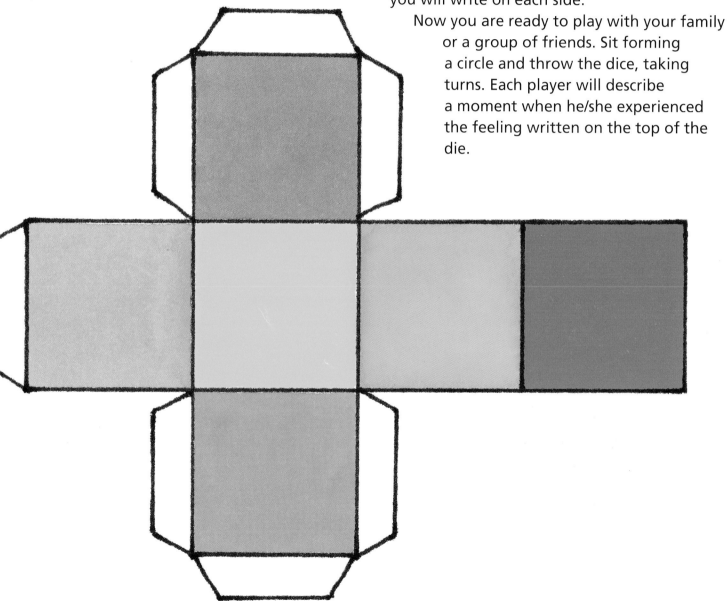

Changing stories

Have you ever tried changing stories? Ask your parents to pretend to have an argument with puppets. Can you now change the story? For example, you may try to find a solution so they will not argue and fight. Now it is your turn to act out a problem and your mom and dad should find the solutions. You will be surprised to find out how many solutions you can think of.

A scary tale

People and things do not always scare us in the same way. Some are very scary and others just a little. We include here a list for you to copy on a piece of oaktag or cardboard using big letters. Ask for some help if you need it! Now you are ready to grade the items on the list. If it scares you, but just a little, you may draw a small ghost next to it. If it scares you some more, then draw a couple of ghosts. And draw three ghosts for those things that really make you feel scared. You can make the list as long as you wish!

Monsters and ghosts
Some animals (wolves, sharks, or others)
Cars
People in costumes
Cookies
An uninhabited house
Clouds
Darkness
Light
Staying alone
Being with people
Aliens
The sun
Some dreams
Cartoons
Loud noise
Music
Falling down
Getting lost
Climbing

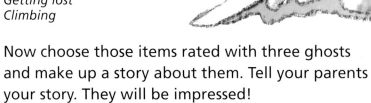

Now choose those items rated with three ghosts and make up a story about them. Tell your parents your story. They will be impressed!

Be an actor

With your mom and dad's help, you can make some cards like these, inventing as many faces as you can think of. It is more fun if you make two or three faces for each feeling. How do you play this game? Shuffle the cards well and hand them out one by one. No player should be able to see what cards the others got. Taking turns, the players act out the feeling on their cards while the others try to guess which feeling it is. The winner is the player who identifies the largest number of feelings. In case you think the game is a little bit difficult, write the name of the feeling under the face illustrated on each card.

Guidelines for parents

Do you know any child who does not ever get mad? There are so many occasions for a child to get mad, often due to the helplessness he/she feels when faced with certain circumstances. It is important to let the child explain what has happened without interrupting him, because if he knows he is being listened to, he will, in turn, learn more easily to do the same. Many children, when they get very mad, choose to stay locked and alone in their room. In this case, respect the child's decision and wait until he calms down. You will eventually be able to talk to him and find out why he got so mad. If the child does not know how to cool off by himself, find the most effective way to help him.

Sometimes, an activity requiring some physical effort may help, such as playing ball, jogging, or jumping. On other occasions, the child may simply prefer to sit down in an isolated corner of the house or in his bedroom. Little by little, the child will learn how to calm down and take it easy before reacting, especially if he sees the way you do it.

Dice of feelings
The activities introduced with the dice and the cards can be useful to help your child identify different feelings and give them a name. When the child hears you talk about how you feel, his vocabulary will become richer and this will make it

easier for him to identify and articulate the feelings he experiences. It is not a question of naming all the feelings you know or explaining the meaning of each term but simply a question of including them in your regular daily comments.

Fear
There are many things that can scare a child or make him feel afraid, but even if you think them unbelievable, you must respect what your child feels. It is never a good idea to tell a child he should not be afraid, because he cannot help feeling that way. However, it is important not to enhance the feeling and to avoid terror movies, scares in the dark, or direct confrontations with the source of fright. If a child is afraid of water and you push him into a swimming pool while he cries and begs you not to, chances are he will forever hate all kinds of aquatic sports. Be very patient and tolerant. Most cases of fear disappear over time, so let your child know that. Also tell him you understand him and stand by his side. Books that offer activities to face fear can be useful, as can the "who is who" guessing game we suggest in the Activities section.

Being afraid is part of a child's learning process, the same as it is with adults. If the problem of fear affects the child's daily life, persists over time, or becomes more intense, check with a specialist. You will be surprised at the number of fear-reducing strategies that exist.

A scary tale
You may adapt the list to your child's personal needs and the activity should always be presented as a game. Don't force the child to continue with the game if he does not feel like it or he does not want to include some of the items in the list. The whole idea is playing with different kinds of fear and making them more understandable, even when they will not disappear entirely.

Be an actor
With this card game, the child can identify feelings but also learn to relate gestures, sounds, facial expressions, and other forms of non-verbal communication to the feeling being expressed. Another game that is fun to play is to imitate well-known people or fictional characters but without costumes: people who are always in a bad mood, or are melancholic.... By means of imitation, children can perceive many different degrees of emotions even if they cannot totally identify them. Through games they can express with words what they could only express in a non-verbal way until recently.

Changing stories
Arguments are not necessarily bad, but many arguments can be avoided if we think calmly. This activity has been designed so your child will be able to start thinking about possible alternatives to avoid conflict, and using puppets will make it easier for him than a direct conversation requiring his personal feelings. Whenever he has an argument, remind him of the game and ask him about the alternatives to avoid the fight. If he cannot think of any, suggest some he could use until he finds the ones he believes are best. Ask him to use them on another similar occasion so he can see for himself if they work or not.

The text talks about feeling sorry and at this early age, children are not aware of the consequences an argument or fight may have, but they do know that things can be broken, like for a favorite toy. The child wishes he had not broken it: that's what is meant by feeling sorry.

And finally...
Fantastic stories, impersonating games, acting out.... Children have many ways to learn about the world around them, not only about the way things are but also their resources to face them. What do adults have? The ability to listen, observe, understand, tolerate...and large amounts of patience. It is not a question of overprotecting your children so they will not experience disagreeable situations, but of being next to them or close by when they experience them. Pain, fear, and sadness are inevitable feelings, but so are happiness, joy, and love. Your child has his own personal characteristics and the more you know him and accept him the way he is, the better you will be able to help him find his own individual resources to face the different situations he encounters along the way.

English language version published by Barron's
Educational Series, Inc., 2001

Original title of the book in Catalan: *Els sentiments: De la
tristesa a la felicitat*
© Copyright GEMSER PUBLICATIONS S.L., 2000
Barcelona, Spain
Author: Núria Roca
Illustrator: Rosa Maria Curto

All inquiries should be addressed to:
Barron's Educational Series, Inc.
250 Wireless Boulevard
Hauppauge, New York 11788
http://www.barronseduc.com

International Standard Book No. 0-7641-1840-4

Library of Congress Catalog Card No. 00-111893

Printed in Spain
9 8 7 6 5 4 3 2 1